ARMORED DINOSAURS
Stegosaurs and Ankylosaurs

Clare Hibbert

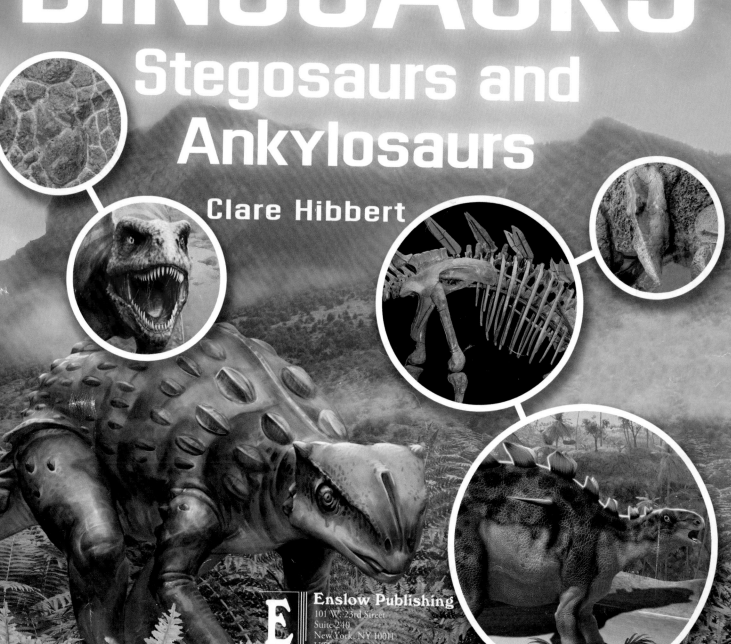

Enslow Publishing
101 W. 23rd Street
Suite 240
New York, NY 10011
USA
enslow.com

Published in 2019 by Enslow Publishing, LLC
101 W. 23rd Street, Suite 240, New York, NY 10011

Cataloging-in-Publication Data

Names: Hibbert, Clare.
Title: Armored dinosaurs: Stegosaurs and Ankylosaurs / Clare Hibbert.
Description: New York : Enslow Publishing, 2019. | Series: Dino explorers | Includes glossary
and index.
Identifiers: ISBN 9780766099876 (pbk.) | ISBN 9780766099869 (library bound) | ISBN
9781978500020 (6 pack.) | ISBN 9780766099883 (ebook)
Subjects: LCSH: Ornithischia--Juvenile literature. | Dinosaurs--Juvenile literature.
Classification: LCC QE862.O65 H53 2019 | DDC 567.915--dc23

Printed in the United States of America

To Our Readers: We have done our best to make sure all website addresses
in this book were active and appropriate when we went to press. However,
the author and the publisher have no control over and assume no
liability for the material available on those websites or on any websites
they may link to. Any comments or suggestions can be sent by email to
customerservice@enslow.com.

Excerpts and articles have been reproduced with the permission of the
copyright holders.

CONTENTS

The Dinosaur Age

Dinosaurs appeared around 225 million years ago (mya) and ruled the land for over 160 million years. At the same time (the Mesozoic Era), marine reptiles and pterosaurs ruled the oceans and skies.

This family tree shows when various dinosaurs appeared and and how they were related. As new fossils are found, paleontologists often change their minds about the groupings.

Dinosaurs suddenly died out 65 mya, along with marine reptiles, pterosaurs and many other animals. A huge meteorite probably hit Earth, throwing up dust that blocked out the Sun for months.

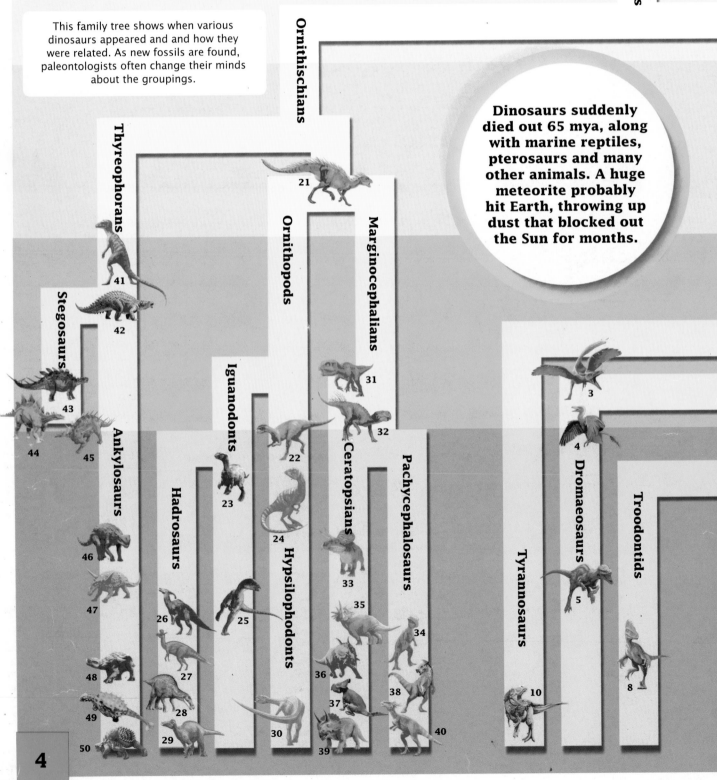

Dinosaurs

Ornithischians

Thyreophorans

Ornithopods

Marginocephalians

Stegosaurs

Ankylosaurs

Hadrosaurs

Iguanodonts

Hypsilophodonts

Ceratopsians

Pachycephalosaurs

Tyrannosaurs

Dromaeosaurs

Troodontids

KEY

1. *Herrerasaurus*
2. *Allosaurus*
3. *Archaeopteryx*
4. *Microraptor*
5. *Deinonychus*
6. *Spinosaurus*
7. *Giganotosaurus*
8. *Troodon*
9. *Therizinosaurus*
10. *Tyrannosaurus*
11. *Melanorosaurus*
12. *Plateosaurus*
13. *Mamenchisaurus*
14. *Brachiosaurus*
15. *Amargasaurus*
16. *Nigersaurus*
17. *Sauroposeidon*
18. *Argentinosaurus*
19. *Saltasaurus*
20. *Rapetosaurus*
21. *Heterodontosaurus*
22. *Hypsilophodon*
23. *Iguanodon*
24. *Leaellynasaura*
25. *Gasparinisaura*
26. *Parasaurolophus*
27. *Lambeosaurus*
28. *Shantungosaurus*
29. *Edmontosaurus*
30. *Thescelosaurus*
31. *Yinlong*
32. *Psittacosaurus*
33. *Zuniceratops*
34. *Stegoceras*
35. *Styracosaurus*
36. *Achelousaurus*
37. *Protoceratops*
38. *Pachycephalosaurus*
39. *Triceratops*
40. *Stygimoloch*
41. *Scutellosaurus*
42. *Scelidosaurus*
43. *Tuojiangosaurus*
44. *Stegosaurus*
45. *Kentrosaurus*
46. *Minmi*
47. *Sauropelta*
48. *Edmontonia*
49. *Euoplocephalus*
50. *Ankylosaurus*

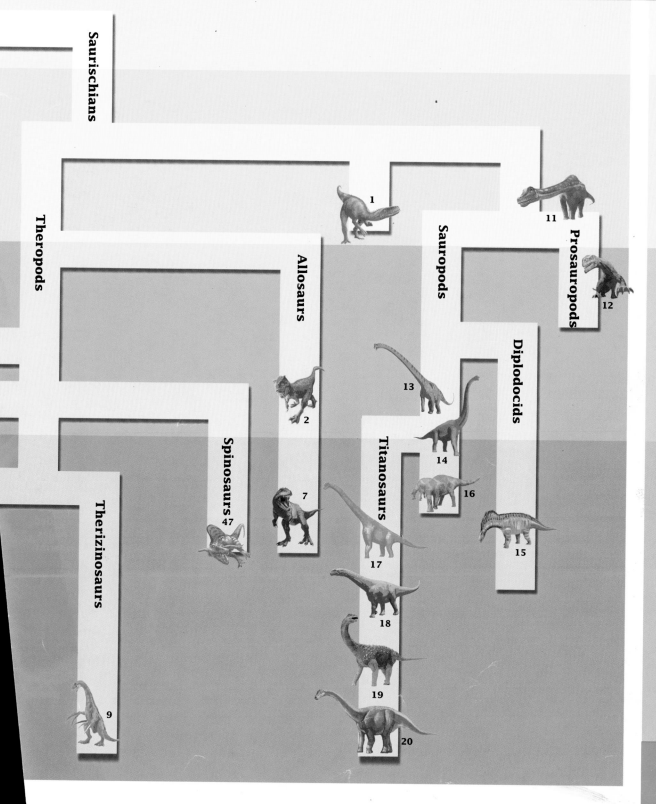

Saurischians

Theropods

Allosaurs

Sauropods

Prosauropods

Spinosaurs

Titanosaurs

Diplodocids

Therizinosaurs

Triassic
251–206 mya

Jurassic
206–145 mya

Cretaceous
145–65 mya

5

Scutellosaurus

Appearing in the Early Jurassic, *Scutellosaurus* was an ancestor of the later shielded dinosaurs, such as *Ankylosaurus* (pages 24–25) and *Stegosaurus* (pages 12–13). The name *Scutellosaurus* means "lizard with little shields."

Little Darter

Scutellosaurus was a plant-eater that lived in what is now Arizona, in the southern United States. Small and lightly built, it had longer back legs than front ones, so it probably moved around on two legs. Its small skull housed a small brain.

The speedy theropod *Coelophysis* would have hunted *Scutellosaurus*.

The Shield Bearers

Scutellosaurus belonged to a group of dinosaurs called the thyreophorans, or "shield bearers." Their skin had evolved to protect them from attack. Early thyreophorans, such as *Scutellosaurus* and *Scelidosaurus* (pages 8–9), simply had bony bumps, called osteoderms. By the Late Cretaceous, the group included ankylosaurs and stegosaurs, which had elaborate plates and spikes.

Scutellosaurus probably went down on all fours to eat shrubby plants.

Scutellosaurus back was stud with bony sc called osteod

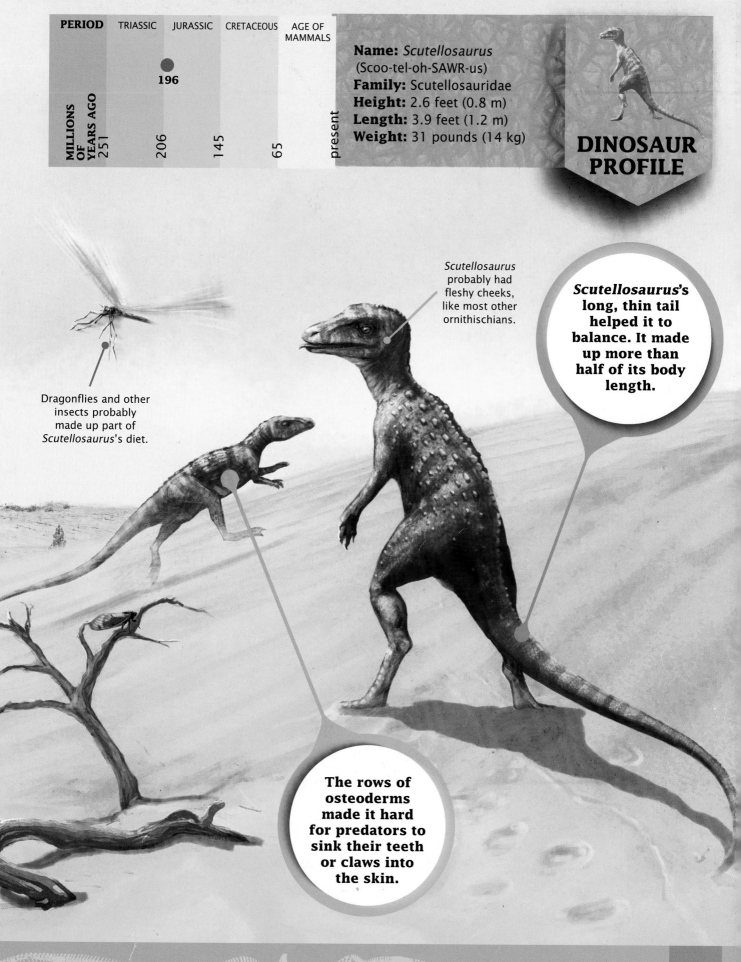

Name: *Scutellosaurus*
(Scoo-tel-oh-SAWR-us)
Family: Scutellosauridae
Height: 2.6 feet (0.8 m)
Length: 3.9 feet (1.2 m)
Weight: 31 pounds (14 kg)

DINOSAUR PROFILE

Scutellosaurus probably had fleshy cheeks, like most other ornithischians.

Scutellosaurus's long, thin tail helped it to balance. It made up more than half of its body length.

Dragonflies and other insects probably made up part of *Scutellosaurus*'s diet.

The rows of osteoderms made it hard for predators to sink their teeth or claws into the skin.

Scelidosaurus

Another of the early thyreophorans, *Scelidosaurus* was discovered in Dorset in southern England. Unlike *Scutellosaurus* (pages 6–7), it walked on all fours. Its bony plates (or scutes) were larger, too—more like those of later dinosaurs in the group.

Teeth and Jaws

Scelidosaurus had a small head, just 7.9 inches (20 cm) long, and a beaky mouth. When it was first found, paleontologists thought it was a fish-eater, because of its long teeth. In reality, it ate plants. Its jaw only moved up and down, not side to side, so it had to bite through leaves rather than grinding them.

Flying reptiles called pterosaurs lived in the Mesozoic.

The beaky mouth was used to eat ferns and conifers.

Legs and Toes

Scelidosaurus was named by Richard Owen, the same scientist who came up with the word "dinosaur." *Scelidosaurus* means "limb lizard" and refers to the dinosaur's stout back legs. The feet had four long toes with blunt claws.

Osteoderms protected the back and tail, but not the legs or underside.

Scelidosaurus had a large stomach for breaking down plant matter.

Scelidosaurus walked on all fours. Its back legs were longer than its front ones, so its head was close to the ground.

This image shows one of the first *Scelidosaurus* finds—an incomplete skull. The snout tip is missing.

PERIOD	TRIASSIC	JURASSIC	CRETACEOUS	AGE OF MAMMALS
MILLIONS OF YEARS AGO	251	206	145	65	present

190

Name: *Scelidosaurus*
(Skel-ee-doe-SAWR-us)
Family: Scelidosauridae
Height: 5 feet (1.5 m)
Length: 13 feet (4 m)
Weight: 595 pounds (270 kg)

DINOSAUR PROFILE

Tuojiangosaurus

Sometimes called the Asian *Stegosaurus* (pages 12–13), *Tuojiangosaurus* lived in China in the Late Jurassic. It was a typical stegosaur, with plates along the length of its back and deadly tail spikes.

Tuojiangosaurus had a double row of horn-covered plates, just like *Kentrosaurus* (pages 14–15).

Sichuan Stegosaurs

Tuojiangosaurus means "Tuo River lizard" after the river in Sichuan Province, southwestern China, where the dinosaur was discovered. Other stegosaurs shared its habitat. Two of these—*Chungkingosaurus* and *Chialingosaurus*, both just 13 feet (4 m) long—may have been *Tuojiangosaurus* juveniles, not separate species.

Tuojiangosaurus held its tail off the ground. It could swing its sharp tail spikes at predators.

PERIOD	TRIASSIC	JURASSIC	CRETACEOUS	AGE OF MAMMALS
MILLIONS OF YEARS AGO	251	206 · 160 / 145	65	present

Name: *Tuojiangosaurus* (Too-YANG-oh-SAWR-us)
Family: Stegosauridae
Height: 6.6 feet (2 m)
Length: 23 feet (7 m)
Weight: 1.7 tons (1.5 t)

DINOSAUR PROFILE

The plates were different sizes and shapes. The largest were over the hip; they grew smaller toward the head.

Eating Habits

Tuojiangosaurus browsed on low plants. While it was eating, its head stayed slightly dipped, helped by the shorter front legs. The jaws contained at least 25 small teeth for snipping off vegetation.

The snout was long and shallow with a beaky tip.

Tuojiangosaurus ate low-growing ferns and cycads.

Early reconstructions of stegosaurs sometimes positioned the front legs sprawling out to the sides. In fact, they were held directly under the body.

Stegosaurus

Stegosaurs are all named after *Stegosaurus*, which ranged across North America and Europe during the Middle Jurassic. This herbivore had a small head, diamond-shaped plates along its back, and a defensive, spiky tail.

Lethal Weapon

The group of spikes at the end of a stegosaur's tail is called a thagomizer. It was *Stegosaurus*'s only protection against predators. The dinosaur swung and flicked its tail, hoping to hit an attacker and inflict serious damage.

Stegosaurus's skull was long and narrow.

Unlike other known stegosaurs, *Stegosaurus*'s plates were staggered instead of in pairs.

All about Plates

Early reconstructions of *Stegosaurus* had its plates flat on top of its body—that is how the dinosaur got its name, which means "roofed lizard." Paleontologists now know that the plates stood upright, making the dinosaur look bigger than it was. They were almost certainly for display, but they may have also helped *Stegosaurus* to regulate its body temperature.

Stegosaurus probably used its plates to show off to other members of the same species.

PERIOD	TRIASSIC	JURASSIC	CRETACEOUS	AGE OF MAMMALS

● 153

MILLIONS OF YEARS AGO

251 | 206 | 145 | 65 | present

Name: *Stegosaurus*
(STEG-uh-SAWR-us)
Family: Stegosauridae
Height: 9 feet (2.7 m)
Length: 30 feet (9.1 m)
Weight: 5.5 tons (5 t)

DINOSAUR PROFILE

Stegosaurus's small skull housed a brain shaped like a hot dog.

Ornitholestes hunted in packs.

Stegosaurus could not move fast because of its short front legs. Its top speed was 4.3 miles per hour (7 km/h).

Ornitholestes was a 27.8-pound (12.6-kg) theropod that lived in North America at the same time as *Stegosaurus*.

Kentrosaurus

The small stegosaur *Kentrosaurus* lived in what is now Tanzania about 152 mya. It shared its wet, swampy forest habitat with one of the giants of the plant-eating dinosaurs, *Giraffatitan*.

Plenty of Plants

There was no shortage of food in Late Jurassic East Africa, so *Kentrosaurus* did not need to compete with *Giraffatitan*. Plants flourished in the wet, tropical climate. *Kentrosaurus* fed low to the ground, using its beaky mouth to snap up vegetation.

As with *Stegosaurus* (pages 12–13), the plates along the back may have helped *Kentrosaurus* lose or soak up heat.

Kentrosaurus had a narrow, pointed snout.

Kentrosaurus's tropical environment had two seasons: dry and wet.

PERIOD	TRIASSIC	JURASSIC	CRETACEOUS	AGE OF MAMMALS
MILLIONS OF YEARS AGO	251	206	145	65	present

152

Name: *Kentrosaurus*
(KEN-truh-SAWR-us)
Family: Stegosauridae
Height: 6 feet (1.8 m)
Length: 15 feet (4.5 m)
Weight: 1.1 tons (1 t)

DINOSAUR PROFILE

Kentrosaurus could swing its tail back 180 degrees to target an attacker alongside its own body.

From Tendaguru

Kentrosaurus was discovered in the Tendaguru Formation. No complete skeleton has been found, but paleontologists have been able to piece different specimens together. They have found nearly a thousand *Kentrosaurus* fossils in the Tendaguru rock.

More than half of *Kentrosaurus*'s body length was made up of its tail.

Minmi

The small ankylosaur *Minmi* lived in what is now Queensland, Australia, around 115 mya. It is named after Minmi Crossing, a landmark near the place where it was first discovered in 1964.

Speed and Shields

Unlike most slow-moving ankylosaurs, *Minmi* was probably a fast runner. It had extra bones across its spine that could have anchored extra muscles. If that really is what those "paravertebrae" (across bones) were for, *Minmi* could have outrun many predators. When it encountered a speedy hunter, it relied on its protective plates to discourage them from attacking.

Minmi had long legs for an ankylosaur.

All-Over Protection

Most ankylosaurs had short, stubby legs. This meant that their softer-skinned bellies were held low to the ground, where they were hard to reach. *Minmi* was different. It had relatively long legs, but it also had bony plates all over its body, even on its underside.

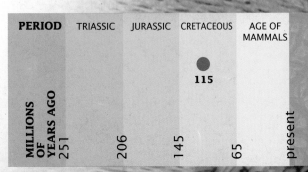

PERIOD	TRIASSIC	JURASSIC	CRETACEOUS	AGE OF MAMMALS

115

MILLIONS OF YEARS AGO

251   206   145   65   present

Name: *Minmi*
(MIN-mee)
Family: Ankylosauridae
Height: 3.3 feet (1 m)
Length: 9.8 feet (3 m)
Weight: 661 lb (300 kg)

DINOSAUR PROFILE

Early Cretaceous Queensland was an island, cut off from the rest of Australia.

Minmi lived in forests and floodplains. It ate ferns, and leaves, fruit, and seeds from the first flowering plants.

Protective plates covered its back and belly.

The skull was shaped like an arrowhead.

Minmi had strong back legs for sprinting through the undergrowth.

Sauropelta

Living across North America in the Early Cretaceous, plant-eating *Sauropelta* was a kind of ankylosaur. Large, bony studs, called osteoderms, shielded its back. Two long, defensive spikes stuck out from its shoulders and it had shorter spikes along its sides.

Well-Defended

Sauropelta means "shielded lizard." Its bones and spikes were essential protection against the predators of the day, such as *Acrocanthosaurus*, a relative of *Allosaurus*, and *Deinonychus*. Even with their fearsome jaws, *Sauropelta*'s studded skin was too hard to bite through.

Nodosaurs

Sauropelta is the earliest known nodosaur. Named after *Nodosaurus*, the tank-like nodosaurs were ankylosaurs that did not have tail clubs but that had certain other features, including a bony bump over each eye, another bump at the base of the skull, and spikes on the lower jaw. *Edmontonia* (pages 20–21) was a nodosaur, too.

The 3-foot- (90-cm-) long shoulder spikes helped make *Sauropelta* look bigger than it really was.

This section of fossilized *Sauropelta* skin shows the protective, bony osteoderms, or scutes.

The flattened skull was made up of plates that had fused together.

PERIOD	TRIASSIC	JURASSIC	CRETACEOUS	AGE OF MAMMALS
MILLIONS OF YEARS AGO	251	206	145	65	present

108

Name: *Sauropelta*
(SAWR-oh-PEL-tah)
Family: Nodosauridae
Height: 8 feet (2.4 m)
Length: 17.1 feet (5.2 m)
Weight: 1.65 tons (1.5 t)

DINOSAUR PROFILE

The long tail contained more than 40 vertebrae (spine bones) and made up half of the dinosaur's total body length.

Sauropelta's back was covered with bony bumps called osteoderms.

Edmontonia

One of the largest nodosaurs, herbivorous *Edmontonia* lived across North America in the Late Cretaceous. Pyramid-shaped spikes covered its back, while forward-facing shoulder spikes protected the head and neck. Sometimes, these spikes split to create even deadlier forked tips.

Shoulder Power

Edmontonia's shoulder spikes carried on growing throughout its life. They gave some protection if the dinosaur had to charge past an attacking theropod. However, their main purpose was for fighting rivals. *Edmontonia* males probably battled over territory and mates. The ones with larger shoulder spikes would have had more status.

Edmontonia has been found in Canada's Dinosaur Park Formation, along with the ankylosaur *Scolosaurus* (left) and nodosaur *Panoplosaurus* (right).

PERIOD	TRIASSIC	JURASSIC	CRETACEOUS	AGE OF MAMMALS
MILLIONS OF YEARS AGO	251	206	145	65 ... present

72

Name: *Edmontonia* (Ed-mon-TOE-nee-uh)
Family: Nodosauridae
Height: 5.9 feet (1.8 m)
Length: 22 feet (6.7 m)
Weight: 3.3 tons (3 t)

DINOSAUR PROFILE

Stories in Rock

As *Edmontonia* was widespread, its fossils have been found in different rock formations across North America. The first identified *Edmontonia* was discovered in 1928 in Alberta's Edmonton Formation (since renamed the Horseshoe Canyon Formation).

Each shoulder spike was made from strong, dense bone.

Rival *Edmontonia* would barge at each other, shoulder to shoulder.

Edmontonia's skull was about 19.7 inches (50 cm) long. It was protected by osteoderms that had fused together to form a bony helmet.

Euoplocephalus

One of the largest ankylosaurs, plant-eating *Euoplocephalus* had a spike-covered body and a wide, heavy tail club. Its short legs carried its body low to the ground, leaving its vulnerable belly almost impossible for any attacker to reach.

Solo Life

Euoplocephalus lived in what is now Canada during the Late Cretaceous. Most fossils have been found on their own, so paleontologists believe that *Euoplocephalus* was not a herd animal. They think it lived alone, like today's hippopotamus.

Horns poked out from the back of the head.

Most ankylosaurs had four toes on their back feet, but *Euoplocephalus* had just three.

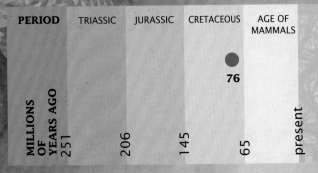

PERIOD	TRIASSIC	JURASSIC	CRETACEOUS	AGE OF MAMMALS
MILLIONS OF YEARS AGO	251	206	145	65 present

76

Name: *Euoplocephalus* (You-op-luh-SEF-uh-lus)
Family: Ankylosauridae
Height: 6 feet (1.8 m)
Length: 20 feet (6 m)
Weight: 2.2 tons (2 t)

DINOSAUR PROFILE

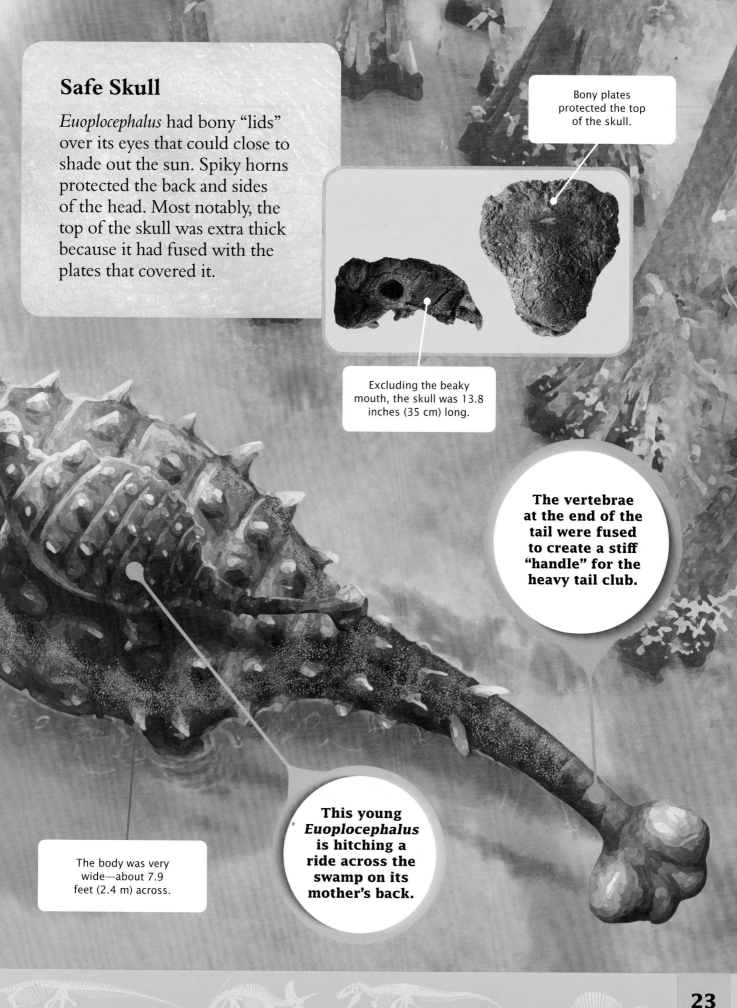

Safe Skull

Euoplocephalus had bony "lids" over its eyes that could close to shade out the sun. Spiky horns protected the back and sides of the head. Most notably, the top of the skull was extra thick because it had fused with the plates that covered it.

Bony plates protected the top of the skull.

Excluding the beaky mouth, the skull was 13.8 inches (35 cm) long.

The vertebrae at the end of the tail were fused to create a stiff "handle" for the heavy tail club.

This young *Euoplocephalus* is hitching a ride across the swamp on its mother's back.

The body was very wide—about 7.9 feet (2.4 m) across.

Ankylosaurus

Ankylosaurs all take their name from *Ankylosaurus* ("fused lizard"). It was the largest ankylosaur and one of the best-protected, with a large tail club of solid bone.

Terrifying Threats

Ankylosaurus lived in North America at the end of the Cretaceous. This herbivore shared its habitat with one of the most terrifying hunters of all time—*Tyrannosaurus*. However, an adult *Ankylosaurus* could have swung its tail club with enough force to break *Tyrannosaurus*'s leg.

Big Head

Ankylosaurus's skull had many air passages running through it that made it bulge out at the sides. Paleontologists are still not sure what these passages were for. They may have helped with the dinosaur's sense of smell or they may have made its calls louder by amplifying them.

Four head spikes protected *Ankylosaurus*'s face.

PERIOD	TRIASSIC	JURASSIC	CRETACEOUS	AGE OF MAMMALS

67

MILLIONS OF YEARS AGO

251 | 206 | 145 | 65 | present

Name: *Ankylosaurus*
(Ang-KILE-uh-SAWR-us)
Family: Ankylosauridae
Height: 5.6 feet (1.7 m)
Length: 20.5 feet (6.2 m)
Weight: 6.6 tons (6 t)

DINOSAUR PROFILE

Hundreds of bite-proof bony plates covered *Ankylosaurus*'s upper body.

Ankylosaurus's jaw housed tiny teeth.

The tail club was made of fused bone.

Fun Facts

Now that you have discovered some stegosaurs and ankylosaurs boost your knowledge with these 10 quick facts about them!

Scutellosaurus is the only known shielded dinosaur that moved around on two legs. The rest were quadrupedal.

In 1858 a *Scelidosaurus* skeleton was found—it was the earliest complete dinosaur fossil.

Tuojiangosaurus was named in 1977. Its fossilized remains had been discovered by construction workers building a dam.

Stegosaurus's plates were up to 2 feet (0.6 m) tall.

Kentrosaurus means "spiked reptile."

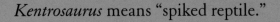

Minmi had the shortest name of any dinosaur for more than two decades. Today, Mei has the shortest name.

Hundreds of fossilized dinosaur footprints discovered in Alberta, Canada, were almost certainly made by herds of *Sauropelta*.

Edmontonia is named after Edmonton, the capital city of the Canadian province of Alberta, in western Canada.

Euoplocephalus had complicated passages in its nose, so it probably had a good sense of smell.

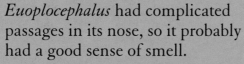

Ankylosaurus had a very large, flexible tongue.

Your Questions Answered

Our scientific knowledge and technologies are constantly improving, which helps paleontologists uncover more and more information about dinosaurs. Each question answered leads to many new ones being asked, and it is the quest of scientists to keep searching for answers to give us the fullest possible picture of prehistoric life. Here are some fascinating questions we can now answer.

How long did dinosaurs live?

Scientists have been able to study the fossilized bones of dinosaurs and work out how long some species lived. They have discovered that large herbivorous dinosaurs probably lived a lot longer than smaller carnivorous ones. While a predator such as *Tyrannosaurus rex* might have lived for 20–30 years, the plant-eating giants like *Diplodocus* probably reached an age of 70–80 years.

The lifespan of **Tyrannosaurus rex** can be compared to that of today's large, flying birds such as eagles or ravens.

What do we know about how dinosaurs defended themselves?

Often scientists can develop theories about how different dinosaurs defended themselves, especially herbivores. But in the case of *Stegosaurus*, fossil evidence has provided more details than usual. Paleontologists had already established that the damage on many *Stegosaurus* thagomizers probably meant the animal used these spikes with some force. Then they discovered an *Allosaurus* fossil that showed traces of serious bone injury. Given the shape of the impact, scientists were able to prove that it had been caused by *Stegosaurus* thagomizers. They may not have always caused bone damage, but at the very least, a brutal club with *Stegosaurus's* tail would have caused a large flesh wound.

What were dinosaurs' plates made of?

Some of the most closely studied dinosaur plates are those of *Stegosaurus*. They were up to 2 feet (0.6 m) tall, and perched upright on the animal's neck, back, and tail. Judging by fossil finds, the plates were made of a bony material, but unlike bones, they weren't solid. Each plate had a network of hollow tubes, which may or may not have housed blood vessels. The outer layer of each plate was a thin coating of horn.

Red deer have antlers that consist of horn—a material that is made of keratin, like our nails and hair.

Are there animals today with osteoderms?

There are a number of animals today that have osteoderms, such as crocodilians (the family that includes crocodiles, alligators, and gharials). The osteoderms line their backs and sometimes stomachs, protecting them from attacks and soaking up the sun's heat. Other animals with osteoderms include many different species of lizard, and a single type of mammal: the armadillo.

The nine-banded armadillo is shielded by its osteoderms. They protect its head, back, legs, and tail.

Glossary

allosaur A large theropod with a long, narrow skull, usually with ornamental horns or crests.

ankylosaur A thyreophoran with defensive osteoderms and, sometimes, a tail club.

browse To feed on shoots, leaves, and other plant matter.

Cretaceous period The time from 145 to 65 mya, and the third of the periods that make up the Mesozoic Era.

fossil The remains of an animal or plant that died long ago, preserved in rock.

herbivore A plant-eater.

Jurassic period The time from 206 to 145 mya, and the second of the periods that make up the Mesozoic Era.

Mesozoic Era The period of geological time from 251 to 65 million years ago.

mya Short for "millions of years ago."

nodosaur An ankylosaur with bumps and spikes on its skull, but no tail club.

ornithischian Describes dinosaurs with hip bones arranged like a bird's. All plant-eaters, they include ornithopods, marginocephalians, and thyreophorans.

osteoderm A lumpy scale on a reptile's skin.

paleontologist A scientist who studies fossils.

plate A protective, bony section on a reptile's skin.

predator An animal that hunts and eats other animals for food.

pterosaur A flying reptile with wings made from skin stretched over a long fourth finger.

quadrupedal Walking on all four legs.

species One particular type of living thing. Members of the same species look similar and can produce offspring together.

stegosaur A thyreophoran with defensive bony plates on its back.

thagomizer The group of defensive spikes on a stegosaur's tail.

theropod A bipedal saurischian dinosaur with sharp teeth and claws.

thyreophoran An ornithischian dinosaur with defensive osteoderms or plates.

Triassic period The time from 251 to 206 mya, and the first of the periods that make up the Mesozoic Era.

tyrannosaur A large theropod with a huge head and relatively small arms.

Further Information

BOOKS

Clay, Kathryn. *Ankylosaurus and Other Armored Dinosaurs: The Need-to-Know Facts.*
North Mankato, MN: Capstone Press, 2016.

Colson, Rob. *Dinosaur Bones: And What They Tell Us.* Buffalo, NY:
Firefly Books, 2016.

Graham, Ian. *The Science of Prehistoric Giants: Dinosaurs That Used Size and Armor for Defense.* New York, NY: Franklin Watts, 2018.

Hulick, Kathryn. *The Science of Dinosaurs.* Minneapolis, MN: Abdo
Publishing, 2016.

WEBSITES

discoverykids.com/category/dinosaurs/
This Discovery Kids site has tons of awesome information about dinosaurs, plus lots of fun games and exciting videos!

kids.nationalgeographic.com/explore/nature/dinosaurs/
Check out this National Geographic Kids site to learn more about dinosaurs!

www.amnh.org/explore/ology/paleontology
This website by the American Museum for
Natural History is filled with dinosaur quizzes,
information, and activities!

Index